the CHEESE L♥VERS COOKBOOK

Publications International, Ltd.

CONTENTS

PARTY STARTERS

CHILI CHEESE FRIES
Makes 4 servings

1½ pounds ground beef

1 medium onion, chopped

2 cloves garlic, minced

½ cup lager

2 tablespoons chili powder

2 tablespoons tomato paste

Salt and black pepper

1 package (32 ounces) frozen French fries

1 jar (15 ounces) cheese sauce, heated

Sour cream and chopped green onions (optional)

1 Brown beef, onion and garlic in large skillet over medium-high heat 6 to 8 minutes, stirring to break up meat. Drain fat.

2 Stir lager, chili powder and tomato paste into beef mixture. Simmer, stirring occasionally, 20 minutes or until most liquid has evaporated. Season with salt and pepper.

3 Meanwhile, bake the French fries according to package directions.

4 Divide the French fries evenly among bowls. Top evenly with chili and cheese sauce. Garnish with sour cream and green onions.

BAKED BUFFALO CHICKEN DIP

Makes 2 cups (about 16 servings)

1 container (8 ounces) cream cheese spread

¼ cup crumbled blue cheese

2 cups chopped cooked chicken breast (about 8 ounces)

3 tablespoons mayonnaise

3 tablespoons sour cream

¼ to ½ cup hot pepper sauce

1 cup (4 ounces) shredded Monterey Jack cheese

2 tablespoons panko bread crumbs

Assorted vegetable sticks and/or pita chips

1 Preheat oven to 400°F. Spray 1-quart casserole with nonstick cooking spray.

2 Combine cream cheese and blue cheese in medium saucepan; heat over medium heat until melted. Remove from heat. Stir in chicken, mayonnaise, sour cream and hot pepper sauce until combined.

3 Spread chicken mixture in prepared dish. Sprinkle with Monterey Jack cheese; top evenly with panko. Spray with cooking spray.

4 Bake 20 minutes or until lightly browned and heated through. Serve with assorted vegetable sticks and/ or pita chips.

MOZZARELLA STICKS

Makes 4 to 6 servings

¼ cup all-purpose flour

2 eggs

1 tablespoon water

1 cup plain dry bread crumbs

2 teaspoons Italian seasoning

½ teaspoon salt

½ teaspoon garlic powder

1 package (12 ounces) string cheese (12 sticks)

Vegetable oil for frying

1 cup marinara or pizza sauce, heated

1 Place flour in shallow bowl. Whisk eggs and water in another shallow bowl. Combine bread crumbs, Italian seasoning, salt and garlic powder in third shallow bowl.

2 Coat each piece of cheese with flour. Dip in egg mixture, letting excess drip back into bowl. Roll in bread crumb mixture to coat. Dip again in egg mixture and roll again in bread crumb mixture. Refrigerate until ready to cook.

3 Heat 2 inches of oil in large saucepan over medium-high heat to 350°F; adjust heat to maintain temperature. Add cheese sticks; cook about 1 minute or until golden brown. Drain on wire rack. Serve with warm marinara sauce for dipping.

QUICK AND EASY ARANCINI

Makes 12 arancini (6 servings)

1 **package (6 to 8 ounces) mushroom or Milanese risotto mix, plus ingredients to prepare mix***

½ **cup frozen peas** *or* **¼ cup finely chopped oil-packed sun-dried tomatoes (optional)**

½ **cup panko bread crumbs**

¼ **cup finely shredded or grated Parmesan cheese**

2 **tablespoons minced fresh parsley**

2 **tablespoons butter, melted**

4 **ounces Swiss, Asiago or fontina cheese, cut into 12 cubes (about ½ inch)**

*Or use 3 cups leftover risotto.

1 Prepare risotto according to package directions. Stir in peas, if desired. Let stand, uncovered, 20 minutes or until thickened and cool enough to handle.

2 Preheat oven to 375°F. Spray 12 standard (2½-inch) muffin pan cups with nonstick cooking spray. Combine panko, Parmesan, parsley and melted butter in medium bowl.

3 Shape level ¼ cupfuls risotto into balls around Swiss cheese cubes, covering completely. Roll in panko mixture to coat. Place in prepared muffin cups.

4 Bake 15 minutes or until arancini are golden brown and cheese cubes are melted. Cool in pan 5 minutes. Serve warm.

GOAT CHEESE CROSTINI WITH SWEET ONION JAM

Makes 24 crostinis (about 12 servings)

1 tablespoon olive oil

2 medium yellow onions, thinly sliced

¾ cup dry red wine

¼ cup water

2 tablespoons packed brown sugar

1 tablespoon balsamic vinegar

1 teaspoon salt

¼ teaspoon black pepper

2 ounces soft goat cheese

2 ounces cream cheese, softened

1 teaspoon chopped fresh thyme, plus additional for garnish

1 loaf (16 ounces) French bread, cut into 24 slices (about 1 inch thick), lightly toasted

1 Heat oil in large skillet over medium heat. Add onions; cook and stir 10 minutes. Add wine, water, brown sugar, vinegar, salt and pepper; bring to a simmer. Reduce heat to low. Cook, uncovered, 15 to 20 minutes or until all liquid is absorbed. (If mixture appears dry, stir in a few tablespoons of additional water.) Cool 30 minutes.

2 Meanwhile, stir goat cheese, cream cheese and 1 teaspoon thyme in small bowl until well blended. Spread ½ teaspoon goat cheese mixture on each slice of bread. Top with 1 teaspoon onion jam. Garnish with additional thyme.

CHEESY GARLIC BREAD

Makes 8 to 10 servings

1 loaf (about 16 ounces) Italian bread

½ cup (1 stick) butter, softened

8 cloves garlic, very thinly sliced

¼ cup grated Parmesan cheese

2 cups (8 ounces) shredded mozzarella cheese

1 Preheat oven to 425°F. Line large baking sheet with foil.

2 Cut bread in half horizontally. Spread cut sides of bread evenly with butter; top with sliced garlic. Sprinkle with Parmesan, then mozzarella cheeses. Place on prepared baking sheet.

3 Bake 12 minutes or until cheeses are melted and golden brown in spots. Cut crosswise into slices. Serve warm.

BAKED BRIE WITH NUT CRUST

Makes 8 servings

⅓ **cup pecans**

⅓ **cup almonds**

⅓ **cup walnuts**

1 **egg**

1 **tablespoon whipping cream**

1 **round (8 ounces) Brie cheese**

2 **tablespoons raspberry jam**

1 Preheat oven to 350°F. Place nuts in food processor fitted with steel blade; pulse to finely chop. *Do not overprocess.* Transfer chopped nuts to shallow dish or pie plate.

2 Combine egg and cream in another shallow dish; whisk until well blended.

3 Dip Brie into egg mixture, then into nut mixture, turning to coat. Press nuts to adhere.

4 Transfer Brie to small baking sheet; spread jam over top. Bake 15 minutes or until cheese is warm and soft.

WARM GOAT CHEESE ROUNDS

Makes 4 servings

1 **package (4 ounces) goat cheese**

1 **egg**

1 **tablespoon water**

⅓ **cup seasoned dry bread crumbs**

1 Cut goat cheese crosswise into 8 slices. (If cheese is too difficult to slice, shape scant tablespoonfuls of cheese into balls and flatten into ¼-inch-thick rounds.)

2 Beat egg and water in small bowl. Place bread crumbs in shallow dish. Dip goat cheese rounds into egg mixture, then in bread crumbs, turning to coat all sides. Gently press bread crumbs to adhere. Place coated rounds on plate; freeze 10 minutes.

3 Cook goat cheese rounds in medium nonstick skillet over medium-high heat 2 minutes per side or until golden brown. Serve immediately.

SERVING SUGGESTIONS: Serve goat cheese rounds with heated marinara sauce or over mixed greens tossed with vinaigrette dressing.

BACON SHRIMP QUESADILLAS

Makes 4 quesadillas

1 tablespoon olive oil

1 small green or red bell pepper, diced

½ pound medium shrimp (26-30 count), cooked, peeled, deveined, diced

3 tablespoons ORTEGA® Enchilada Sauce

½ teaspoon ground cumin

Salt and black pepper, to taste

8 (8-inch) ORTEGA® Flour Soft Tortillas

8 strips bacon, cooked, crumbled

1 cup (4 ounces) coarsely grated Monterey Jack cheese

1 cup ORTEGA® Thick & Chunky Salsa

1 cup ORTEGA® Guacamole Style Dip

HEAT oil in large nonstick skillet over medium-high heat until hot. Add bell pepper. Cook and stir 2 to 3 minutes. Add shrimp, enchilada sauce, cumin, and salt and pepper, to taste. Cook and stir until golden and just cooked through, about 2 minutes.

HEAT large nonstick skillet over medium-high heat until hot. Coat with nonstick cooking spray. Place one tortilla in skillet. Spoon one-fourth of bacon, ¼ cup cheese and one-fourth of shrimp mixture evenly over tortilla. Top with second tortilla and press down firmly.

COOK until golden brown and crisp on bottom, about 2 to 3 minutes. Carefully turn over. Cook until golden on other side, 2 to 3 minutes longer. Transfer to cutting board and cut into wedges. Repeat with remaining ingredients.

SERVE with salsa and guacamole dip.

CHEESY FONDUE

Makes 4 servings

2 cups (8 ounces) shredded Swiss cheese

2 cups (8 ounces) shredded Monterey Jack cheese

2 tablespoons all-purpose flour

1½ cups dry white wine or apple juice

Dash ground nutmeg

Dash ground red pepper

1 French bread loaf, cut into cubes

1 large Granny Smith apple, cut into wedges, or other fruit pieces

1 Combine cheeses and flour in large bowl; toss lightly to coat.

2 Bring wine to a simmer over medium heat in fondue pot. Gradually add cheese mixture until melted, stirring constantly. Stir in nutmeg and red pepper. Serve with bread cubes and apple for dipping. Keep warm, stirring occasionally.

TACO BOULDERS

Makes 12 biscuits

2¼ cups biscuit baking mix

1 cup (4 ounces) shredded taco cheese blend

2 tablespoons canned diced mild green chiles, drained

⅔ cup milk

3 tablespoons butter, melted

¼ teaspoon chili powder

¼ teaspoon garlic powder

1 Preheat oven to 425°F. Line baking sheet with parchment paper or spray with nonstick cooking spray.

2 Combine baking mix, cheese and chiles in large bowl. Stir in milk just until moistened. Drop dough by ¼ cupfuls into 12 mounds on prepared baking sheet.

3 Bake 11 to 13 minutes or until golden brown. Meanwhile, combine butter, chili powder and garlic powder in small bowl. Remove biscuits to wire rack; immediately brush with butter mixture. Serve warm.

POTATO SKINS

8 medium baking potatoes (6 to 8 ounces each)

1 tablespoon vegetable oil

1 teaspoon salt

⅛ teaspoon black pepper

1 tablespoon butter, melted

1 cup (4 ounces) shredded Cheddar cheese

8 slices bacon, crisp-cooked and coarsely chopped

1 cup sour cream

3 tablespoons snipped fresh chives

1 Preheat oven to 400°F.

2 Prick potatoes all over with fork. Rub oil over potatoes; sprinkle with salt and pepper. Place in 13×9-inch baking pan. Bake 1 hour or until fork-tender. Let stand until cool enough to handle. *Reduce oven temperature to 350°F.*

3 Cut potatoes in half lengthwise; cut small slice off bottom of each half so potato halves lay flat. Scoop out soft middles of potato skins; reserve for another use. Place potato halves skin sides up in baking pan; brush potato skins with butter.

4 Bake 20 to 25 minutes or until crisp. Turn potatoes over; top with cheese and bacon. Bake 5 minutes or until cheese is melted. Cool slightly. Top with sour cream and chives just before serving.

GRILLED FETA WITH PEPPERS

Makes 8 servings

- ¼ **cup thinly sliced sweet onion**
- 1 **package (8 ounces) feta cheese, sliced in half horizontally**
- ¼ **cup thinly sliced green bell pepper**
- ¼ **cup thinly sliced red bell pepper**
- ½ **teaspoon dried oregano**
- ¼ **teaspoon garlic pepper or black pepper**
- **Sliced French bread (optional)**

1 Spray 14-inch-long sheet of foil with nonstick cooking spray. Place onion slices in center of foil and top with feta slices. Sprinkle with bell pepper slices, oregano and garlic pepper.

2 Seal foil using Drugstore Wrap technique (*See tip below*). Place foil packet on grid upside down and grill on covered grill over hot coals 15 minutes. Turn packet over; grill on covered grill 15 minutes more.

3 Open packet carefully and serve immediately with slices of French bread.

DRUGSTORE WRAP: Place food in the center of an oblong piece of heavy-duty foil, leaving at least a 2-inch border around the food. Bring two long sides together above the food; fold down in a series of locked folds, allowing for heat circulation and expansion. Fold short ends up and over again. Press folds firmly to seal the foil packet.

MAC & CHEESE BITES

Makes about 2 dozen

3 packages (3 ounces each) ramen noodles, any flavor, divided*

8 ounces pasteurized process cheese product

1 cup (4 ounces) shredded Cheddar cheese

1 teaspoon salt

½ teaspoon ground red pepper

Vegetable oil

Discard seasoning packets.

1 Prepare 2 packages ramen according to package directions; drain and return to saucepan.

2 Stir in cheese product, Cheddar cheese, salt and ground red pepper. Let stand 10 to 15 minutes.

3 Finely crush remaining packet ramen noodles in food processor or blender. Put crumbs in pie pan. Using hands, shape cheese mixture into 1-inch balls; roll in ramen crumbs. Flatten slightly.

4 Heat about ½ to 1 inch oil in large skillet. Add bites, a few at a time; cook 1½ minutes per side until golden brown. Remove from skillet; drain on paper towels.

GOAT CHEESE, CARAMELIZED ONIONS AND PROSCIUTTO FLATBREAD BITES

Makes 6 servings

- 2 tablespoons olive oil, plus additional for drizzling
- 1 large onion, sliced
- ¼ teaspoon salt
- ¼ cup water
- All-purpose flour, for dusting
- 1 package (about 14 ounces) refrigerated pizza dough
- 2 ounces goat cheese
- 4 slices prosciutto
- ½ teaspoon fresh thyme sprigs

1 Preheat oven to 450°F. Line baking sheet with parchment paper.

2 Heat 2 tablespoons oil in large skillet over medium heat. Add onion and salt; cook 18 to 20 minutes or until onion is deep golden brown, stirring occasionally and adding water halfway through cooking. Set aside to cool slightly.

3 Roll out dough into two 9×5-inch rectangles on lightly floured surface. Transfer dough to prepared baking sheet; top with onion, goat cheese and prosciutto.

4 Bake 12 minutes or until crust is golden brown and prosciutto is crisp. Drizzle with additional oil and sprinkle with thyme. Cut each flatbread into 12 portions.

CARAMELIZED ONION FOCACCIA

- **2** tablespoons plus 1 teaspoon olive oil, divided
- **1** loaf (16 ounces) frozen bread dough, thawed
- **4** onions
- **½** teaspoon salt
- **2** tablespoons water
- **1** tablespoon chopped fresh rosemary
- **¼** teaspoon black pepper
- **1** cup (4 ounces) shredded fontina cheese
- **¼** cup grated Parmesan cheese

1 Brush 13×9-inch baking pan with 1 teaspoon oil. Roll out dough into 13×9-inch rectangle on lightly floured surface. Place in prepared pan; cover and let rise in warm place 30 minutes.

2 Spiral onions using fine spiral blade or slicing blade; cut into desired lengths.

3 Heat remaining 2 tablespoons oil in large skillet over medium-high heat. Add onions and salt; cook 10 minutes or until onions begin to brown, stirring occasionally. Stir in water. Reduce heat to medium; partially cover and cook 20 minutes or until onions are deep golden brown, stirring occasionally. Remove from heat; stir in rosemary and pepper. Let cool slightly.

4 Preheat oven to 375°F. Prick dough all over (about 12 times) with fork. Sprinkle fontina cheese over dough; top with caramelized onions. Sprinkle with Parmesan cheese.

5 Bake 18 to 20 minutes or until golden brown. Remove from pan to wire rack. Cut into pieces; serve warm.

CHEESY CHICKEN NACHOS

Makes 6 servings

2 tablespoons olive oil

1 onion, diced

1 teaspoon POLANER® Chopped Garlic

1 pound ground chicken

1 jar (16 ounces) ORTEGA® Salsa, any variety, divided

2 teaspoons dried parsley flakes

1 teaspoon ORTEGA® Chili Seasoning Mix

1 teaspoon REGINA® Red Wine Vinegar

½ cup water

12 ORTEGA® Yellow Corn Taco Shells, broken

4 cups (16 ounces) shredded taco cheese blend

1 can (15 ounces) ORTEGA® Black Beans, rinsed, drained

1 jar (12 ounces) ORTEGA® Sliced Jalapeños

HEAT oil in skillet over medium-high heat until hot. Add onion and garlic. Cook and stir until onions are translucent, about 3 minutes. Stir in chicken, ¾ cup salsa, parsley, seasoning mix, vinegar and water; cook until meat is cooked through and sauce begins to thicken, about 5 minutes.

PREHEAT broiler; place rack about 7 inches from top of oven.

ASSEMBLE nachos by arranging broken taco shells on baking sheet. Sprinkle on 2 cups cheese; top evenly with chicken mixture, beans and jalapeños. Add remaining salsa and cheese. (If desired, prepare individual portions by dividing recipe among 6 heat-resistant plates.)

PLACE under broiler 4 minutes or until cheese begins to melt.

TIP: Make the nachos even tastier by topping them with sour cream, B&G® Sliced Ripe Olives and ORTEGA® Guacamole Style Dip.

TIP: If you have ground beef on hand, you can still make these tasty nachos. Just brown the meat first and discard the excess fat before proceeding as directed. Or try this recipe with ground turkey.

HOT "CRAB" AND ARTICHOKE DIP

Makes 6 to 8 servings

1 (8-ounce) package cream cheese, softened

½ cup mayonnaise

½ cup shredded Cheddar cheese

¼ cup CREAM OF WHEAT® Hot Cereal (Instant, 1-minute, 2½-minute or 10-minute cook time), uncooked

1 teaspoon TRAPPEY'S® Red Devil™ Cayenne Pepper Sauce

1 teaspoon Worcestershire sauce

1 teaspoon Chesapeake seasoning

1 (9-ounce) jar artichoke hearts, drained, coarsely chopped

8 ounces pasteurized surimi (imitation crabmeat), coarsely chopped

1 teaspoon ground paprika

Vegetables, crackers or tortilla chips (optional)

1 Preheat oven to 350°F. Stir cream cheese in medium mixing bowl until softened. Add mayonnaise, Cheddar cheese, Cream of Wheat, pepper sauce, Worcestershire sauce and Chesapeake seasoning; mix well. Fold in artichoke hearts and surimi.

2 Pour into 1-quart casserole dish. Sprinkle on paprika. Bake 30 minutes. Serve warm with vegetables, crackers or tortilla chips, if desired.

VARIATION: Spread dip on English muffins, and place under the broiler for a few minutes until bubbly and browned. Cut into quarters and serve.

CRUNCHY PARMESAN ZUCCHINI STICKS

Makes 6 appetizer servings

3 medium zucchini

1 package (3 ounces) ramen noodles, any flavor

½ cup shredded Parmesan cheese

½ cup all-purpose flour

1 egg

1 tablespoon water

Prepared marinara sauce for dipping

1 Preheat oven to 400°F. Line baking sheet with parchment paper. Cut zucchini in half crosswise, then cut each half into 4 sticks.

2 Place noodles and cheese in food processor or blender; pulse until fine crumbs form. Pour into shallow dish.

3 Place flour and ramen seasoning packet in another shallow dish; stir to combine. Whisk egg and water in third shallow dish. Line dishes up for dipping.

4 First dip zucchini stick in flour, then egg, then noodle mixture. Place on prepared baking sheet. Repeat with remaining zucchini and ingredients.

5 Bake 20 minutes or until zucchini is softened and coating is golden brown. Serve warm with marinara sauce for dipping.

BELL PEPPER NACHOS

Makes 8 servings

1 green bell pepper

1 yellow or red bell pepper

2 Italian plum tomatoes, seeded and finely chopped

⅓ cup finely chopped onion

1 teaspoon chili powder

½ teaspoon ground cumin

1½ cups cooked rice

½ cup (2 ounces) shredded Monterey Jack cheese

¼ cup chopped fresh cilantro

2 teaspoons jalapeño pepper sauce *or* ¼ teaspoon hot pepper sauce

½ cup (2 ounces) shredded sharp Cheddar cheese

1 Spray medium baking sheets with nonstick cooking spray. Cut bell peppers into 1-inch triangles; set aside.

2 Spray large skillet with cooking spray. Add tomatoes, onion, chili powder and cumin; cook and stir over medium heat 3 minutes or until onion is tender. Remove from heat. Stir in rice, Monterey Jack cheese, cilantro and jalapeño pepper sauce.

3 Top each pepper triangle with about 2 tablespoons rice mixture; sprinkle with Cheddar cheese. Place on prepared baking sheets; cover and refrigerate 1 hour or up to 8 hours.

4 When ready to serve, preheat broiler. Remove plastic wrap. Broil nachos 6 to 8 inches from heat 3 to 4 minutes (or bake at 400°F 8 to 10 minutes) or until cheese is bubbly and rice is heated through.

OOEY GOOEY SANDWICHES

BACON & TOMATO MELTS
Makes 4 sandwiches

- 8 slices bacon, crisp-cooked
- 8 slices (1 ounce each) Cheddar cheese
- 2 tomatoes, sliced
- 8 slices whole grain bread
- ¼ cup (½ stick) butter, melted

1 Layer 2 slices bacon, 2 slices cheese and tomato slices on each of 4 bread slices; top with remaining bread slices. Brush sandwiches with butter.

2 Heat grill pan or large skillet over medium heat. Add sandwiches; press lightly with spatula or weigh down with small plate. Cook 4 to 5 minutes per side or until cheese is melted and sandwiches are golden brown.

PIZZA SANDWICH
Makes 4 to 6 servings

1 loaf (12 ounces) focaccia

½ cup pizza sauce

20 slices pepperoni

8 slices (1 ounce each) mozzarella cheese

1 can (2¼ ounces) sliced mushrooms, drained

Red pepper flakes (optional)

Olive oil

1 Cut focaccia horizontally in half. Spread cut sides of both halves with pizza sauce. Layer bottom half with pepperoni, cheese and mushrooms; sprinkle with red pepper flakes, if desired. Cover with top half of focaccia. Brush sandwich lightly with oil.

2 Heat large nonstick skillet over medium heat. Add sandwich; press down with spatula or weigh down with small plate. Cook sandwich 4 to 5 minutes per side or until cheese is melted and sandwich is golden brown. Cut into wedges to serve.

NOTE: Focaccia can be found in the bakery section of most supermarkets. It is often available in different flavors, such as tomato, herb, cheese or onion.

HAVARTI & ONION SANDWICHES

Makes 2 sandwiches

1½ teaspoons olive oil

⅓ cup thinly sliced red onion

4 slices pumpernickel bread

6 ounces dill havarti cheese, cut into slices

½ cup prepared coleslaw

1 Heat oil in large skillet over medium heat. Add onion; cook and stir 5 minutes or until tender. Layer 2 bread slices with onion, cheese and coleslaw; top with remaining 2 bread slices.

2 Heat same skillet over medium heat. Add sandwiches; press down with spatula or weigh down with small plate. Cook 4 to 5 minutes on each side or until cheese is melted and sandwiches are browned.

PEAR GORGONZOLA MELTS

Makes 4 sandwiches

4 ounces creamy Gorgonzola cheese (do not use crumbled blue cheese)

8 slices walnut raisin bread

2 pears, cored and sliced

½ cup fresh spinach leaves

Butter, melted

1 Spread cheese evenly on 4 bread slices; layer with pears and spinach. Top with remaining bread slices. Brush outsides of sandwiches with butter.

2 Heat large nonstick skillet over medium heat. Add sandwiches; cook 4 to 5 minutes per side or until cheese is melted and sandwiches are golden brown.

AWESOME GRILLED CHEESE SANDWICHES

Makes 3 servings

1 package (11.25 ounces) Pepperidge Farm® Garlic Texas Toast

6 slices fontina cheese or mozzarella cheese

6 thin slices deli smoked turkey

3 thin slices prosciutto

1 jar (12 ounces) sliced roasted red pepper, drained

1 Heat a panini or sandwich press according to the manufacturer's directions until hot. (Or, use a cast-iron skillet or ridged grill pan.)

2 Top **3** of the bread slices with **half** of the cheese, turkey, prosciutto, peppers and remaining cheese. Top with the remaining bread slices.

3 Put the sandwiches on the press, closing the lid onto the sandwiches. Cook the sandwiches for 5 minutes (if cooking in a skillet or grill pan, press with a spatula occasionally or weigh down with another cast-iron skillet/foil-covered brick), until lightly browned and the bread is crisp and the cheese melts.

KITCHEN TIP: For a spicier flavor, add a dash of crushed red pepper flakes on the cheese when assembling the sandwiches.

TUSCAN PORTOBELLO MELT

Makes 2 servings

1 **portobello mushroom cap, thinly sliced**

½ **small red onion, thinly sliced**

½ **cup grape tomatoes**

1 **tablespoon olive oil**

1 **teaspoon balsamic vinegar**

⅛ **teaspoon salt**

⅛ **teaspoon dried thyme**

⅛ **teaspoon black pepper**

2 **tablespoons butter, softened and divided**

4 **slices sourdough bread**

2 **slices provolone cheese**

2 **teaspoons Dijon mustard**

2 **slices Monterey Jack cheese**

1 Preheat broiler. Combine mushroom, onion and tomatoes in small baking pan. Drizzle with oil and vinegar; sprinkle with salt, thyme and pepper. Toss to coat. Spread vegetables in single layer in pan.

2 Broil 6 minutes or until vegetables are softened and browned, stirring once.

3 Heat medium skillet over medium heat. Spread 1 tablespoon butter over one side of each bread slice. Place buttered side down in skillet; cook 2 minutes or until bread is toasted. Transfer bread to cutting board, toasted sides up.

4 Place provolone cheese on 2 bread slices; spread mustard over cheese. Top with vegetables, Monterey Jack cheese and remaining bread slices, toasted sides down. Spread remaining 1 tablespoon butter on outside of sandwiches. Cook in same skillet over medium heat 5 minutes or until bread is toasted and cheese is melted, turning once.

CHEESY CHICKEN
AND BACON MELTS

Makes 4 servings

8 slices bacon

2 cloves garlic, crushed

4 boneless skinless chicken breasts (about 1 pound)

⅛ teaspoon salt

⅛ teaspoon black pepper

1 tablespoon prepared pesto

4 wheat French rolls, split

12 fresh spinach leaves

8 fresh basil leaves* (optional)

3 plum tomatoes, sliced

½ cup (2 ounces) shredded mozzarella cheese

Omit basil leaves if fresh are unavailable. Do not substitute dried basil leaves.

1 Preheat oven to 350°F. Heat large skillet over medium-high heat. Add bacon; cook and turn until crisp-cooked. Remove bacon to paper towel-lined plate. Set aside.

2 Remove all but 1 tablespoon bacon drippings from skillet. Heat over medium heat. Rub garlic on all surfaces of chicken. Add chicken; cook 5 to 6 minutes on each side or until no longer pink in center. Sprinkle with salt and pepper.

3 Brush pesto sauce onto bottom halves of rolls; layer with spinach, basil, if desired, and tomatoes. Place chicken in rolls; sprinkle cheese evenly over chicken. Top with bacon. (If desired, sandwiches may be prepared up to this point and wrapped in foil. Refrigerate until ready to bake. Bake in preheated 350°F oven until chicken is warm, about 20 minutes.)

4 Wrap sandwiches in foil; bake 10 minutes or until cheese is melted.

GRILLED PESTO, RAMEN AND CHEESE SANDWICH

Makes 4 servings

1 package (3 ounces) ramen noodles, any flavor*

¼ cup prepared pesto

8 slices French or Italian bread

4 slices provolone cheese

1 tomato, cut into slices

3 tablespoons butter, divided

Discard seasoning packet.

1 Prepare noodles according to package directions; rinse and drain well. Place noodles in medium bowl; add pesto, stirring to mix well.

2 Divide noodle mixture among 4 slices bread. Top each with 1 slice cheese, 2 slices tomato and remaining bread slices.

3 Heat 1½ tablespoons butter in grill pan or heavy skillet over medium heat. Cook 2 sandwiches, 3 minutes per side, until sandwiches are golden brown and cheese is melted. Repeat with remaining 2 sandwiches.

BACON AND CHEESE RAREBIT

Makes 6 servings

- 1½ tablespoons butter
- ½ cup lager (not dark beer)
- 2 teaspoons Worcestershire sauce
- 2 teaspoons Dijon mustard
- ⅛ teaspoon ground red pepper
- 2 cups (8 ounces) shredded American cheese
- 1½ cups (6 ounces) shredded sharp Cheddar cheese
- 1 small loaf (8 ounces) egg bread or challah, cut into 6 (1-inch-thick) slices
- 12 large slices tomato
- 12 slices bacon, crisp-cooked
- Finely chopped fresh thyme (optional)

1 Preheat broiler. Line medium baking sheet with foil.

2 Melt butter in double boiler set over simmering water. Stir in lager, Worcestershire sauce, mustard and red pepper; cook until heated through, stirring occasionally. Gradually add cheeses, stirring constantly until melted. Remove from heat; cover and keep warm.

3 Broil bread slices until golden brown. Arrange on prepared baking sheet. Top each serving with tomato and bacon. Spoon about ¼ cup cheese sauce evenly over each serving. Broil 4 to 5 inches from heat just until cheese sauce begins to brown. Garnish with thyme.

MINI CHEDDAR-
BEER BISCUITS WITH HAM

Makes 12 servings (2 biscuits each)

2 cups all-purpose flour

1 tablespoon baking powder

½ teaspoon salt

1 cup (about 4 ounces) shredded Cheddar cheese

¼ cup shortening

¾ cup lager

1 egg, lightly beaten

8 slices cooked ham*

1 tablespoon honey mustard

Use your favorite deli ham.

1 Preheat oven to 425°F. Grease baking sheet. Combine flour, baking powder and salt in large bowl. Stir in cheese. Cut in shortening with pastry blended or two knives until mixture resembles coarse crumbs. Add lager; stir just until combined.

2 Divide dough in half. Pat half of dough on prepared baking sheet into 6×4½-inch rectangle, about ½ inch thick. Score dough into 12 squares. Repeat with remaining dough.

3 Brush top of dough with egg. Bake 17 minutes or until golden brown. Cool on baking sheet 2 minutes. Remove to wire rack; cool completely.

4 Cut 1 rectangle horizontally. Arrange 4 slices of ham to cover biscuit bottom. Spread 1½ teaspoons mustard on underside of biscuit top; place on ham. Repeat with second rectangle of biscuits, remaining ham and mustard. Cut along score lines into 24 individual biscuits.

THE GREAT REUBEN SANDWICH

Makes 2 sandwiches

- ¼ cup Thousand Island dressing (see Tip)
- 4 slices rye bread
- 8 ounces thinly sliced corned beef or pastrami
- 4 slices Swiss cheese
- ½ cup sauerkraut, well drained
- 2 tablespoons butter

1 Spread dressing on one side of each bread slice. Top 2 bread slices with corned beef, cheese, sauerkraut and remaining bread slices.

2 Melt butter in large skillet over medium heat. Add sandwiches; press down with spatula or weigh down with small plate. Cook 6 minutes per side or until cheese is melted and bread is lightly browned. Serve immediately.

TIP: If you don't have Thousand Island dressing, you can make your own by combining 2 tablespoons mayonnaise, 2 tablespoons sweet pickle relish and 1 tablespoon cocktail sauce.

GRILLED CHEESE KABOBS

Makes 12 servings

8 thick slices whole wheat bread

3 thick slices sharp Cheddar cheese

3 thick slices Monterey Jack or Colby Jack cheese

2 tablespoons butter, melted

1 Cut each slice bread into 1-inch squares. Cut each slice cheese into 1-inch squares. Make small sandwiches with one square of bread and one square of each type of cheese. Top with second square of bread.

2 Brush sandwiches with melted butter. Heat nonstick grill pan over medium-high heat. Grill sandwich kabobs 30 seconds on each side or until golden and cheese is slightly melted. Skewer each sandwich with short wooden skewer to remove them from the skillet.

GRILLED CHEESE, HAM & ONION MELTS

Makes 4 servings

1 tablespoon butter or margarine

2 medium onions, thinly sliced

1 teaspoon sugar

⅓ cup FRENCH'S® Honey Dijon Mustard

16 slices Muenster cheese

12 slices deli ham

8 slices rye bread

1 Melt butter in medium nonstick skillet. Add onions. Cook over medium-high heat until tender, stirring often. Reduce heat to medium-low. Stir in sugar; cook 15 to 20 minutes or until onions are caramelized. Stir in mustard and remove from heat.

2 Place 2 slices cheese and 3 slices ham on each of 4 slices of bread. Spoon ¼ cup onion mixture over ham. Top with 2 more slices cheese and cover with remaining bread slices.

3 Coat an electric grill pan with nonstick cooking spray. Grill sandwiches about 5 minutes until golden and cheese melts.

TIP: Sandwiches may be cooked in a nonstick skillet or on an outdoor grill.

TIP: Substitute deli roast beef for ham.

SPICY CHEESEBURGER SLIDERS

Makes 8 sliders

1 pound Ground Beef (96% lean)

9 small whole wheat hamburger buns, split, divided

1 clove garlic, minced

½ teaspoon ground chipotle chili powder

2 slices pepper jack cheese, cut in quarters

TOPPINGS:

Barbecue sauce, lettuce, tomato slices, pickles (optional)

1 Tear one hamburger bun into pieces. Place in food processor or blender container. Cover; pulse on and off, to form fine crumbs.

2 Combine bread crumbs, beef, garlic and chili powder in medium bowl, mixing lightly but thoroughly. Lightly shape into eight ½-inch thick mini patties.

3 Place patties on grill over medium, ash-covered coals. Grill, covered, 8 to 9 minutes (over medium heat on preheated gas grill, 9 to 10 minutes) until instant-read thermometer inserted horizontally into center registers 160°F, turning occasionally. Evenly top with cheese during last minute of grilling.

4 Place burgers on bottoms of remaining eight buns. Top with desired Toppings. Close sandwiches.

Courtesy The Beef Checkoff

PORTOBELLO & FONTINA SANDWICHES

Makes 2 sandwiches

2 teaspoons olive oil, plus additional for brushing

2 large portobello mushrooms, stems removed

Salt and black pepper

2 to 3 tablespoons sun-dried tomato pesto

4 slices crusty Italian bread

4 ounces fontina cheese, sliced

½ cup fresh basil leaves

1 Preheat broiler. Line baking sheet with foil.

2 Drizzle 2 teaspoons oil over both sides of mushrooms; season with salt and pepper. Place mushrooms, gill sides up, on prepared baking sheet. Broil mushrooms 4 minutes per side or until tender. Cut into ¼-inch-thick slices.

3 Spread pesto evenly on 2 bread slices; layer with mushrooms, cheese and basil. Top with remaining bread slices. Brush outsides of sandwiches lightly with additional oil.

4 Heat large grill pan or skillet over medium heat. Add sandwiches; press down lightly with spatula or weigh down with small plate. Cook 5 minutes per side or until cheese is melted and sandwiches are golden brown.

ARGENTINIAN BEEF MELT

Makes 4 servings

12 ounces cooked beef pot roast or brisket, shredded

1 medium red bell pepper, cut into ¼-inch thick strips

4 slices reduced-fat or regular provolone cheese

4 slices crusty bread (about 6×3×½-inch)

CHIMICHURRI SAUCE:

¾ cup packed fresh parsley, chopped

2 cloves garlic

1 tablespoon fresh lime juice

1 tablespoon olive oil

¼ teaspoon salt

1 Preheat oven to 350°F. Place bread slices in single layer on baking sheet. Place bell pepper strips on foil-lined baking sheet coated with nonstick cooking spray. Bake bread in 350°F oven 10 to 13 minutes, turning once. Roast peppers 10 to 15 minutes or until lightly browned. Set aside.

2 Meanwhile, place parsley and garlic in food processor or blender container. Cover; process until finely chopped. Add lime juice, oil, and salt; process just until blended.

3 Spread Chimichurri Sauce evenly on one side of each bread slice; top evenly with pot roast and red pepper strips. Top each bread slice with cheese. Place on baking sheet. Bake in 350°F oven 7 to 10 minutes or until beef is heated through and cheese is melted.

Variation: *One half cup jarred roasted red peppers, thinly sliced, may be substituted for fresh red bell pepper.*

Courtesy The Beef Checkoff

WAFFLED GRILLED CHEESE

Makes 1 serving

2 **tablespoons butter**

2 **slices bread**

1 **teaspoon mustard**

1 **slice American cheese**

1 **slice ham**

1 Preheat waffle iron to medium. Spread 1 tablespoon butter on one side of each bread slice; spread mustard on other side. Layer cheese and ham over mustard. Top with remaining bread slice, mustard side down.

2 Coat waffle iron lightly with nonstick cooking spray. Place sandwich in waffle iron; close lid. Cook 3 to 5 minutes or until top is browned and cheese is melted.

CLASSIC PATTY MELTS

Makes 4 servings

5 tablespoons butter, divided

2 large yellow onions, thinly sliced

¾ teaspoon plus pinch of salt, divided

1 pound ground chuck (80% lean)

½ teaspoon garlic powder

½ teaspoon onion powder

¼ teaspoon black pepper

8 slices marble rye bread

½ cup Thousand Island dressing

8 slices deli American or Swiss cheese

1 Melt 2 tablespoons butter in large skillet over medium heat. Add onions and pinch of salt; cook 20 minutes or until onions are very soft and golden brown, stirring occasionally. Remove to small bowl; wipe out skillet with paper towel.

2 Combine beef, remaining ¾ teaspoon salt, garlic powder, onion powder and pepper in medium bowl; mix gently. Shape into four patties about the size and shape of bread slices and ¼ to ½ inch thick.

3 Melt 1 tablespoon butter in same skillet over medium-high heat. Add patties, two at a time; cook 3 minutes or until bottoms are browned, pressing down gently to form crust. Turn patties; cook 3 minutes or until browned. Remove patties to plate; wipe out skillet with paper towel.

4 Spread one side of each bread slice with dressing. Top 4 bread slices with cheese slice, patty, caramelized onions, another cheese slice and remaining bread slices.

5 Melt 1 tablespoon butter in same skillet over medium heat. Add two sandwiches to skillet; cook 4 minutes or until golden brown, pressing down to crisp bread. Turn sandwiches; cook 4 minutes or until golden brown and cheese is melted. Repeat with remaining sandwiches and 1 tablespoon butter.

BOWLS & SALADS

FRENCH ONION SOUP

Makes 8 servings

4 tablespoons butter, divided

3 pounds yellow onions, peeled and sliced

1 tablespoon sugar

2 to 3 tablespoons dry white wine or water

2 quarts (8 cups) beef broth

8 to 16 slices French bread

½ cup (2 ounces) shredded Gruyère or Swiss cheese

SLOW COOKER DIRECTIONS

1 Melt butter in large skillet over medium-low heat. Add onions; cover and cook 10 minutes or until onions are transparent.

2 Sprinkle sugar over onions. Cook, covered, 8 to 10 minutes or until onions are caramelized, stirring occasionally. Transfer onions to slow cooker. Add wine to skillet. Bring to a boil, scraping up any browned bits from bottom of skillet. Add to slow cooker. Stir in broth. Cover; cook on LOW 8 hours or on HIGH 6 hours.

3 Preheat broiler. To serve, ladle soup into individual bowls; top with 1 or 2 slices bread and about 1 tablespoon cheese. Place under broiler until cheese is melted and bubbly.

VARIATION: Substitute 1 cup dry white wine for 1 cup of the beef broth.

CHEESY CHICKEN CHILI

Makes 4 servings

- 1½ Tbsp. olive or vegetable oil
- 1 lb. boneless, skinless chicken breast halves, cut into ¾-inch chunks
- 2 Tbsp. ground cumin
- 1 jar (16 oz.) salsa
- 2 cans (16 oz. each) great northern beans, drained and rinsed
- 1 cup frozen corn
- 1½ cups (6 oz.) Sargento® Fine Cut Shredded Colby-Jack Cheese or Sargento® Fine Cut Shredded Monterey Jack Cheese, divided

    Sour cream, sliced green onions, sliced black olives and crushed tortilla chips (optional)

HEAT oil in large saucepan over medium heat. Add chicken; cook 3 minutes, stirring frequently. Add cumin; cook 1 minute, stir constantly. Add salsa, beans and corn; bring to a boil. Reduce heat; cover and simmer 15 minutes, stirring once.

REMOVE from heat; stir in 1 cup cheese. Ladle into bowls; top with remaining cheese and serve with sour cream, green onions, black olives and tortilla chips, as desired.

BEET AND BLUE SALAD

Makes 4 servings

1 package (6 ounces) baby spinach

1 cup sliced beets

½ cup diced red onions

½ cup matchstick carrots

¼ cup balsamic vinegar

2 tablespoons canola oil

2 tablespoons pure maple syrup

¼ teaspoon salt

⅛ teaspoon red pepper flakes

¼ cup crumbled blue cheese

1 Divide spinach equally among four salad plates. Top evenly with beets, onions and carrots.

2 Whisk vinegar, oil, maple syrup, salt and red pepper flakes in small bowl until well blended. Drizzle dressing over salad. Sprinkle evenly with cheese.

TWO-CHEESE POTATO
AND CAULIFLOWER SOUP

Makes 4 to 6 servings

1 tablespoon butter

1 cup chopped onion

2 cloves garlic, minced

5 cups whole milk

1 pound Yukon Gold potatoes, diced

1 pound cauliflower florets

1½ teaspoons salt

⅛ teaspoon ground red pepper

1½ cups (6 ounces) shredded sharp Cheddar cheese

⅓ cup crumbled blue cheese

1 Melt butter in large saucepan over medium-high heat. Add onion; cook and stir 4 minutes or until translucent. Add garlic; cook and stir 15 seconds. Add milk, potatoes, cauliflower, salt and red pepper; bring to a boil. Reduce heat to low. Cover tightly and simmer 15 minutes or until potatoes are tender. Cool slightly.

2 Working in batches, process soup in food processor or blender until smooth. Return to saucepan. Cook and stir over medium heat just until heated through. Remove from heat; stir in cheeses until melted.

TIP: One pound of trimmed cauliflower will yield about 1½ cups of florets. You can also substitute 1 pound of frozen cauliflower florets for the fresh florets.

GREEK NOODLE SALAD

Makes 4 servings

2 packages (3 ounces each) ramen noodles, any flavor, broken in half*

3 tablespoons olive oil

Juice of 1 lemon

2 tablespoons red wine vinegar

1 teaspoon dried oregano

1 cup grape tomatoes, halved

¾ cup diced cucumber

½ cup crumbled feta cheese

¼ cup kalamata olives, slivered

2 tablespoons chopped fresh parsley

Discard seasoning packets.

1 Bring 4 cups water to a boil in large saucepan. Add noodles; boil 2 minutes. Drain and rinse under cold running water.

2 Combine oil, lemon juice, vinegar and oregano in large bowl. Add noodles, tomatoes, cucumber, cheese, olives and parsley; toss to coat.

TIP: This easy-to-prepare salad makes a delicious side for baked or grilled fish.

SWISS ORZO CHOWDER

Makes 4 servings

1¼ cups canned chicken broth

1 cup frozen cut green beans

½ cup shredded carrot

⅓ cup (2 ounces) uncoooked orzo

1 teaspoon dried basil

¼ teaspoon black pepper

½ cup sliced yellow summer squash or zucchini

2½ cups milk, divided

3 tablespoons all-purpose flour

¼ cup (1 ounce) shredded Swiss cheese

1 Combine broth, green beans, carrot, orzo, basil and pepper in medium saucepan. Bring to a boil over high heat; reduce heat to medium-low. Cover; simmer 10 minutes. Add squash. Cover; simmer 2 minutes or until vegetables are tender.

2 Whisk ½ cup milk and flour in small bowl until smooth and well blended. Stir into vegetable mixture. Stir in remaining 2 cups milk; bring to a boil over medium heat, stirring constantly. Boil 1 minute. Stir in cheese; cook and stir until melted.

COBB SALAD TO GO

½ cup blue cheese salad dressing

1 ripe avocado, diced

1 tomato, chopped

6 ounces cooked chicken breast, cut into 1-inch pieces

4 slices bacon, crisp-cooked and crumbled *or* ½ cup bacon bits

2 hard-cooked eggs, mashed

1 large carrot, shredded

½ cup blue cheese, crumbled

1 package (10 ounces) torn mixed salad greens

1 Place 2 tablespoons salad dressing into bottom of four (1-quart) jars. Layer remaining ingredients on top, ending with salad greens. Seal jars.

2 Refrigerate until ready to serve.

CREAMY ONION SOUP

Makes 4 servings

6 tablespoons (¾ stick) butter, divided

1 large sweet onion, thinly sliced (about 3 cups)

1 can (about 14 ounces) chicken broth

2 cubes chicken bouillon

¼ teaspoon black pepper

¼ cup all-purpose flour

1½ cups milk

1½ cups (6 ounces) shredded Colby-Jack cheese

Chopped fresh parsley (optional)

1 Melt 2 tablespoons butter in large saucepan or Dutch oven over medium heat. Add onions; cook 10 minutes or until soft and translucent, stirring occasionally. Add broth, bouillon and pepper; cook until bouillon is dissolved and mixture is heated through.

2 Meanwhile, melt remaining 4 tablespoons butter in medium saucepan. Whisk in flour; cook and stir 1 minute. Gradually whisk in milk until well blended. Cook 10 minutes or until very thick, stirring occasionally.

3 Add milk mixture to soup; cook over medium-low heat 5 to 10 minutes or until thickened, stirring occasionally. Add cheese; cook 5 minutes or until melted and smooth. Ladle into bowls; garnish with parsley.

CHEESY WALDORF SALAD

Makes 6 to 8 servings

⅓ cup mayonnaise

1 tablespoon honey

1 tablespoon cider vinegar

4 small *or* 3 large apples, cored and cut into ½-inch pieces (about 4 cups)

4 ounces provolone cheese, cubed

2 stalks celery, thinly sliced

½ cup walnuts or pecans, toasted* and chopped, divided

Red leaf lettuce leaves

To toast walnuts, cook and stir in small skillet over medium heat 1 to 2 minutes or until lightly browned.

1 Combine mayonnaise, honey and vinegar in large bowl until blended. Add apples, cheese, celery and ¼ cup walnuts; stir to coat. (At this point the salad may be refrigerated up to 8 hours.)

2 To serve, line individual salad plates with lettuce, then top with salad. Sprinkle remaining ¼ cup walnuts over each serving.

BAKED POTATO SOUP

Makes 6 to 8 servings

3 medium russet potatoes (about 1 pound)

¼ cup (½ stick) butter

1 cup chopped onion

½ cup all-purpose flour

4 cups chicken or vegetable broth

1½ cups instant mashed potato flakes

1 cup water

1 cup half-and-half

1 teaspoon salt

½ teaspoon dried basil

½ teaspoon dried thyme

¼ teaspoon black pepper

1 cup (4 ounces) shredded Cheddar cheese

4 slices bacon, crisp-cooked and crumbled

1 green onion, chopped

1 Preheat oven to 400°F. Scrub potatoes and prick in several places with fork. Place in baking pan; bake 1 hour. Cool completely; peel and cut into ½-inch pieces. (Potatoes can be prepared several days in advance; refrigerate until ready to use.)

2 Melt butter in large saucepan or Dutch oven over medium heat. Add onion; cook and stir 3 minutes or until softened. Whisk in flour; cook and stir 1 minute. Gradually whisk in broth until well blended. Stir in mashed potato flakes, water, half-and-half, salt, basil, thyme and pepper; bring to a boil over medium-high heat. Reduce heat to medium; cook 5 minutes.

3 Stir in baked potato cubes; cook 10 to 15 minutes or until soup is thickened and heated through. Ladle into bowls; top with cheese, bacon and green onion.

WEDGE SALAD

Makes 4 servings

DRESSING

¾ **cup mayonnaise**

½ **cup buttermilk**

1 **cup crumbled blue cheese, divided**

1 **clove garlic, minced**

½ **teaspoon sugar**

⅛ **teaspoon onion powder**

⅛ **teaspoon salt**

⅛ **teaspoon ground black pepper**

SALAD

1 **head iceberg lettuce**

1 **large tomato, diced (about 1 cup)**

½ **small red onion, cut into thin rings**

½ **cup crumbled crisp-cooked bacon (6 to 8 slices)**

1 For dressing, combine mayonnaise, buttermilk, ½ cup cheese, garlic, sugar, onion powder, salt and pepper in food processor or blender; process until smooth.

2 For salad, cut lettuce into quarters through stem end; remove stem from each wedge. Place wedges on individual serving plates; top with dressing. Sprinkle with tomato, onion, remaining ½ cup cheese and bacon.

GREEK SALAD BOWL

Makes 4 servings

1 cup uncooked pearled farro

2½ cups water

1¼ teaspoons dried oregano or Greek seasoning, divided

½ teaspoon salt, divided

¼ cup extra virgin olive oil

2 tablespoons red wine vinegar

1 clove garlic, minced

⅛ teaspoon black pepper (optional)

2 cucumbers, julienned, cubed or thinly sliced

½ red onion, thinly sliced

2 medium tomatoes, diced

1 can (about 15 ounces) chickpeas, rinsed and drained

4 ounces feta cheese, cubed or crumbled

1 Rinse farro under cold running water; place in medium saucepan. Add 2½ cups water, 1 teaspoon oregano and ¼ teaspoon salt. Bring to a boil over high heat. Reduce heat to medium-low; simmer, uncovered, 20 minutes or until farro is tender. Drain any additional water.

2 Whisk oil, vinegar, garlic, remaining ¼ teaspoon salt, remaining ¼ teaspoon oregano and pepper, if desired, in small bowl.

3 Divide farro among four bowls; arrange cucumber, onion, tomatoes, chickpeas and feta around farro. Drizzle with dressing.

NOTE: This bowl is a great make-ahead option for lunches or future dinners. Add some grilled chicken or lamb for a heartier meal, or mix everything together and serve it as a side dish.

NOTE: This is a great recipe to use a spiralizer if you have one. Cut the ends off the cucumbers and spiral slice with the thin ribbon blade. Spiral the red onion with the thin ribbon blade and chop into desired pieces.

BROCCOLI CHEESE SOUP

Makes 4 to 6 servings

6 tablespoons (¾ stick) butter

1 cup chopped onion

1 clove garlic, minced

¼ cup all-purpose flour

2 cups vegetable broth

2 cups milk

1½ teaspoons Dijon mustard

½ teaspoon salt

¼ teaspoon ground nutmeg

¼ teaspoon black pepper

⅛ teaspoon hot pepper sauce

1 package (16 ounces) frozen broccoli (5 cups)

2 carrots, shredded (1 cup)

6 ounces pasteurized process cheese product, cubed

1 cup (4 ounces) shredded sharp Cheddar cheese, plus additional for garnish

1 Melt butter in large saucepan or Dutch oven over medium-low heat. Add onion; cook and stir 10 minutes or until softened. Add garlic; cook and stir 1 minute. Increase heat to medium. Whisk in flour until smooth; cook and stir 3 minutes without browning.

2 Gradually whisk in broth and milk. Add mustard, salt, nutmeg, black pepper and hot pepper sauce; cook 15 minutes or until thickened.

3 Add broccoli; cook 15 minutes. Add carrots; cook 10 minutes or until vegetables are tender.

4 Transfer half of soup to food processor or blender; process until smooth. Return to saucepan. Add cheese product and 1 cup Cheddar; cook and stir over low heat until cheese is melted. Ladle into bowls; garnish with additional Cheddar.

POTATO & SPINACH SOUP WITH GOUDA

Makes 8 to 10 servings

6 cups cubed peeled Yukon Gold potatoes (about 9 medium)

2 cans (about 14 ounces each) chicken broth

½ cup water

1 small red onion, finely chopped

5 ounces baby spinach

½ teaspoon salt

¼ teaspoon ground red pepper

¼ teaspoon black pepper

2½ cups (10 ounces) shredded smoked Gouda cheese, divided

1 can (12 ounces) evaporated milk

1 tablespoon olive oil

4 cloves garlic, cut into thin slices

Chopped fresh parsley

SLOW COOKER DIRECTIONS

1 Combine potatoes, broth, water, onion, spinach, salt, red pepper and black pepper in slow cooker. Cover; cook on LOW 10 hours or on HIGH 4 to 5 hours.

2 Slightly mash potatoes in slow cooker; add 2 cups cheese and evaporated milk. Cover; cook on HIGH 15 to 20 minutes or until cheese is melted.

3 Heat oil in small skillet over low heat. Add garlic; cook and stir 2 minutes or until golden brown. Remove from heat. Sprinkle soup with garlic, remaining ½ cup cheese and parsley.

TIP: Yukon Gold potatoes are thin-skinned, pale yellow-gold potatoes with pale yellow flesh. When buying potatoes, make sure there are no bruises, sprouts or green areas. Store Yukon Golds in a cool, dark place and use within 1 week of purchase.

FRESH TOMATO AND MOZZARELLA SALAD

Makes 4 servings

Vinaigrette Dressing (recipe follows)

1 **pound fresh mozzarella cheese**

1 **pound ripe tomatoes**

Fresh basil leaves

Salt and black pepper

Prepare Vinaigrette Dressing. Cut mozzarella into ¼-inch slices. Cut tomatoes into ¼-inch slices. Arrange mozzarella slices, tomato slices and basil leaves overlapping on plate. Drizzle with dressing. Sprinkle with salt and pepper.

VINAIGRETTE DRESSING

Makes about ¼ cup

1 **tablespoon balsamic vinegar or red wine vinegar**

¼ **teaspoon Dijon mustard**

Pinch *each* sugar, salt and black pepper

¼ **cup extra virgin olive oil**

Combine vinegar, mustard, sugar, salt and pepper in small bowl; whisk until smooth. Add oil in thin stream, whisking until smooth. Refrigerate until ready to use. Whisk again before serving.

GREEK PASTA SALAD IN A JAR

PASTA SALAD

- 6 cups cooked regular or multigrain rotini pasta
- 1½ cups diced cucumber
- 1 cup diced tomatoes (about 2 medium)
- 1 cup diced green bell pepper (about 1 medium)
- 1 package (4 ounces) crumbled feta cheese
- 12 medium pitted black olives, sliced
- ¼ cup chopped fresh dill

DRESSING

- ¼ cup olive oil
- ¼ cup lemon juice
- ¼ teaspoon salt
- ¼ teaspoon dried oregano
- ⅛ teaspoon black pepper

1 For pasta salad, combine pasta, cucumber, tomatoes, bell pepper, feta cheese, olives and dill in large bowl.

2 For dressing, combine oil, lemon juice, salt, oregano and black pepper in small bowl. Pour over pasta salad; toss well to coat.

3 If desired, spoon about 2 cups pasta salad into each of six (1-pint) resealable jars. Seal jars. Refrigerate until ready to serve.

SHERRIED OYSTER
AND BRIE SOUP

Makes 4 servings

1 cup cream sherry

1 quart select Maryland oysters with liquor

2 tablespoons butter

1 pound mushrooms, thinly sliced

½ cup minced shallots

2 tablespoons fresh lemon juice

2 tablespoons all-purpose flour

3 cups beef broth

4 ounces Brie cheese

1 cup milk

1 cup whipping cream

Salt and white pepper

Fresh snipped chives (optional)

1 Bring sherry to a boil in small saucepan over medium-high heat. Reduce heat to low. Simmer until slightly thickened and reduced to ½ cup. Set aside.

2 Drain oysters, reserving liquor. Set aside.

3 Melt butter in large saucepan over medium-high heat. When foam subsides, stir in mushrooms, shallots and lemon juice; cook and stir 2 minutes. Sprinkle with flour; cook and stir 1 minute.

4 Add broth and reduced sherry; bring to a boil. Reduce heat to low. Simmer 20 minutes.

5 Cut Brie cheese into wedges; using paring knife, remove and discard outer white rind.

6 Add cheese to soup; stir to melt. Stir in reserved oyster liquor, milk and cream; season to taste with salt and pepper. Heat until very hot. *Do not boil.* Remove from heat; add oysters. Cover; let stand until oysters are just plumped. Garnish with fresh chives.

MEATY MAIN DISHES

CHEESY CHICKEN ENCHILADAS VERDE

Makes 4 servings

1 jar (16 ounces) Pace® Salsa Verde

1½ cups shredded cooked chicken

½ cup sour cream

6 ounces shredded Cheddar Jack cheese (about 1½ cups)

8 corn tortillas or flour tortillas (6-inch), warmed

1 Heat the oven to 375°F. Spread **½ cup** salsa verde in a 2-quart shallow baking dish.

2 Stir **¼ cup** salsa verde, chicken, sour cream and **½ cup** cheese in a medium bowl. Spoon **about 3 tablespoons** of the chicken mixture down the center of **each** tortilla. Roll up and place seam-side down in the baking dish. Top with the remaining salsa verde.

3 Bake for 15 minutes. Top with the remaining cheese and bake for 5 minutes or until the cheese is melted.

CHICKEN PARMESAN STROMBOLI

Makes 6 servings

1 pound boneless, skinless chicken breast halves

½ teaspoon salt

¼ teaspoon ground black pepper

2 teaspoons olive oil

2 cups shredded mozzarella cheese (about 8 ounces)

1 jar (1 pound 8 ounces) RAGÚ® Chunky Pasta Sauce, divided

2 tablespoons grated Parmesan cheese

1 tablespoon finely chopped fresh parsley

1 pound fresh or thawed frozen bread dough

1 Preheat oven to 400°F. Season chicken with salt and pepper. In 12-inch skillet, heat olive oil over medium-high heat and brown chicken. Remove chicken from skillet and let cool; pull into large shreds.

2 In medium bowl, combine chicken, mozzarella cheese, ½ cup Ragú Chunky Pasta Sauce, Parmesan cheese and parsley; set aside.

3 On greased jelly-roll pan, press dough to form 12×10-inch rectangle. Arrange chicken mixture down center of dough. Cover filling bringing one long side into center, then overlap with the other long side; pinch seam to seal. Fold in ends and pinch to seal. Arrange on pan, seam-side down. Gently press in sides to form 12×4-inch loaf. Bake 35 minutes or until dough is cooked and golden. Cut stromboli into slices. Heat remaining pasta sauce and serve with stromboli.

CHICKEN RICOTTA ENCHILADAS

Makes 4 servings

⅛ teaspoon garlic powder

⅛ teaspoon black pepper

1 pound chicken tenders

1 cup ricotta cheese

2 tablespoons finely chopped green onion

8 (6-inch) corn tortillas

¼ cup chicken broth

1 large tomato, chopped

½ cup chipotle salsa or other salsa

½ cup (2 ounces) shredded mozzarella cheese

Sprigs fresh parsley or cilantro (optional)

1 Preheat oven to 450°F. Spray 13×9-inch baking dish with nonstick cooking spray.

2 Combine garlic powder and pepper in small bowl; sprinkle evenly over chicken. Spray large skillet with cooking spray; heat over medium-high heat. Add chicken; cook, without stirring, 4 minutes or until golden. Turn chicken; cook 4 minutes or until no longer pink in center.

3 Combine ricotta cheese and green onion in small bowl; mix well. Spray large skillet with cooking spray; heat over medium heat. Heat tortillas, one at a time, in medium skillet over medium heat about 15 seconds per side.

4 Spread ricotta mixture across middle of warm tortillas; place chicken on top. Roll up tortillas; place seam side down in prepared baking dish. Drizzle broth evenly over top. Combine tomato and salsa in small bowl. Spoon over enchiladas; top with mozzarella cheese.

5 Bake, covered, 15 minutes or until heated through and cheese is melted. Garnish with parsley.

BAKED PASTA AND CHEESE SUPREME

Makes 4 servings

8 ounces uncooked fusilli pasta or other corkscrew-shaped pasta

12 slices bacon, chopped

½ medium onion, chopped

2 cloves garlic, minced

2 teaspoons dried oregano, divided

1 can (8 ounces) tomato sauce

1 teaspoon hot pepper sauce (optional)

1½ cups (6 ounces) shredded Cheddar or Colby cheese

½ cup fresh bread crumbs (from 1 slice of white bread)

1 tablespoon butter, melted

1 Preheat oven to 400°F. Cook pasta according to package directions; drain. Meanwhile, cook bacon in large ovenproof skillet over medium heat until crisp. Drain on paper towels; set aside.

2 Add onion, garlic and 1 teaspoon oregano to skillet; cook and stir 3 minutes or until onion is translucent. Stir in tomato sauce and hot pepper sauce, if desired. Add pasta and cheese; stir to coat.

3 Combine bacon, bread crumbs, remaining 1 teaspoon oregano and butter in small bowl; sprinkle over pasta mixture. Bake 10 to 15 minutes or until hot and bubbly.

THAT'S ITALIAN MEAT LOAF

Makes 8 servings

- 1 **can (8 ounces) tomato sauce, divided**
- 1 **egg, lightly beaten**
- ½ **cup chopped onion**
- ½ **cup chopped green bell pepper**
- ⅓ **cup seasoned dry bread crumbs**
- 2 **tablespoons grated Parmesan cheese**
- ½ **teaspoon garlic powder**
- ¼ **teaspoon black pepper**
- 1 **pound ground beef**
- ½ **pound ground pork**
- 1 **cup (4 ounces) shredded Asiago cheese**

SLOW COOKER DIRECTIONS

1 Reserve ⅓ cup tomato sauce; refrigerate. Combine remaining tomato sauce and egg in large bowl. Stir in onion, bell pepper, bread crumbs, Parmesan cheese, garlic powder and black pepper. Add ground beef and pork; mix well. Shape beef mixture into loaf.

2 Carefully transfer meat loaf to slow cooker. Cover; cook on LOW 8 to 10 hours or on HIGH 4 to 6 hours (internal temperature should read 170°F).

3 Spread meat loaf with reserved tomato sauce; sprinkle with Asiago cheese. Cover; cook on HIGH 15 minutes or until cheese is melted.

TIP: To present the whole meat loaf at the table, make foil handles from three 18×2-inch strips of heavy-duty foil (or use regular foil folded to double thickness). Crisscross foil strips in spoke design and place in slow cooker before adding meat loaf. Use foil handles to remove finished meat loaf when fully cooked.

CHICKEN BROCCOLI
RICE CASSEROLE
Makes 4 to 6 servings

3 cups cooked long grain rice

4 boneless skinless chicken breasts (about 1 pound), cooked and cut into 1-inch pieces

1½ pounds broccoli, cut into 1-inch pieces and steamed until tender

2 cans (10¾ ounces each) condensed cream of celery soup, undiluted

¾ cup mayonnaise

½ cup whole milk

2 teaspoons curry powder

3 cups (12 ounces) shredded sharp Cheddar cheese

1 Preheat oven to 350°F. Grease 13×9-inch baking dish.

2 Spread cooked rice evenly into prepared dish. Top with chicken and broccoli. Mix soup, mayonnaise, milk and curry powder in medium bowl; pour over chicken and broccoli. Top with cheese.

3 Cover loosely with foil. Bake 45 minutes or until cheese is melted and casserole is heated through.

BAKED PENNE & HAM

Makes 4 servings

1 package (18 ounces) white sauce mix

2 cups milk

1½ cups (6 ounces) shredded fontina cheese, divided

3 cups cooked penne pasta (2 cups uncooked)

2 cups FRENCH'S® French Fried Onions, divided

1 cup diced boiled ham

½ cup frozen peas

⅓ cup chopped oil-packed sun-dried tomatoes, drained

1 Prepare white sauce mix according to package directions using 2 cups milk. Stir in 1 cup cheese. Cook over low heat, stirring constantly, until cheese melts.

2 Combine pasta, 1 cup French Fried Onions, ham, peas and tomatoes in large bowl. Add cheese sauce and toss to coat. Transfer to shallow 2-quart microwave-safe dish.

3 Microwave, covered, on HIGH 5 minutes. Stir. Sprinkle with remaining onions and cheese. Microwave on HIGH 3 minutes or cheese is melted and onions are golden.

BLUE CHEESE STUFFED CHICKEN BREASTS

Makes 4 servings

½ cup crumbled blue cheese

2 tablespoons butter, softened, divided

¾ teaspoon dried thyme

Salt and black pepper

4 bone-in skin-on chicken breasts

1 tablespoon lemon juice

1 Preheat oven to 400°F. Combine cheese, 1 tablespoon butter and thyme in small bowl; mix well. Season with salt and pepper.

2 Loosen chicken skin by pushing fingers between skin and meat, taking care not to tear skin. Spread cheese mixture under skin; massage skin to spread mixture evenly over chicken breast. Place in shallow roasting pan.

3 Melt remaining 1 tablespoon butter in small bowl; stir in lemon juice until blended. Brush mixture over chicken. Sprinkle with salt and pepper.

4 Roast 50 minutes or until chicken is cooked through (165°F).

CHEESY CHICKEN & POTATO CASSEROLE

Makes 6 servings

1 package (28 ounces) hash brown potatoes with onions and peppers, thawed

1 can (10½ ounces) Campbell's® Condensed Cream of Chicken Soup or Campbell's® Condensed 98% Fat Free Cream of Chicken Soup

1 cup sour cream

2 cups shredded Cheddar cheese or Colby Jack cheese

½ cup milk

½ teaspoon garlic powder

¼ teaspoon ground black pepper

¼ teaspoon salt

3 cups shredded cooked chicken

4 slices bacon, cooked and crumbled

2 tablespoons chopped fresh chives or thinly sliced green onion

1 Heat the oven to 375°F. Spray a 13×9×2-inch baking dish with vegetable cooking spray. Season potatoes as desired.

2 Stir the soup, sour cream, **1 cup** cheese, milk, garlic powder and black pepper in a medium bowl.

3 Spread the potatoes in the baking dish. Season the potatoes with the salt and additional black pepper. Top with the chicken. Spread the soup mixture over the chicken. Cover the baking dish.

4 Bake for 40 minutes or until the potatoes are tender and the mixture is hot and bubbling. Uncover the baking dish. Sprinkle with the remaining cheese.

5 Bake, uncovered, for 5 minutes or until the cheese is melted. Sprinkle with the bacon and chives before serving.

AUSSIE CHICKEN

Makes 4 servings

½ cup honey

½ cup Dijon mustard

2 tablespoons vegetable oil, divided

1 teaspoon lemon juice

4 boneless skinless chicken breasts (about 1½ pounds)

Salt and black pepper

1 tablespoon butter

2 cups sliced mushrooms

4 slices bacon, cooked

½ cup (2 ounces) shredded Cheddar cheese

½ cup (2 ounces) shredded Monterey Jack cheese

Chopped fresh parsley

1 Whisk honey, mustard, 1 tablespoon oil and lemon juice in medium bowl until well blended. Remove half of marinade mixture to use as sauce; cover and refrigerate until ready to serve.

2 Place chicken in large resealable food storage bag. Pour remaining half of marinade over chicken; seal bag and turn to coat. Refrigerate at least 2 hours.

3 Preheat oven to 375°F. Remove chicken from marinade; discard marinade. Heat remaining 1 tablespoon oil in large ovenproof skillet over medium-high heat. Add chicken; cook 3 to 4 minutes per side or until golden brown. (Chicken will not be cooked through.) Remove chicken to plate; sprinkle with salt and pepper.

4 Heat butter in same skillet over medium-high heat. Add mushrooms; cook 8 minutes or until mushrooms begin to brown, stirring occasionally and scraping up any browned bits from bottom of skillet. Season with salt and pepper. Return chicken to skillet; spoon mushrooms over chicken. Top with bacon; sprinkle with Cheddar and Monterey Jack cheeses.

5 Bake 8 to 10 minutes or until chicken is no longer pink in center and cheeses are melted. Sprinkle with parsley; serve with reserved honey-mustard mixture.

PULLED PORK QUESADILLAS

Makes 8 servings

1 **pound pork tenderloin, cut into 3-inch pieces**

1 **cup beer**

1 **cup barbecue sauce**

1 **teaspoon chili powder**

4 **(8-inch) flour tortillas**

2⅔ **cups shredded Monterey jack cheese**

Salsa, sour cream and fresh cilantro leaves (optional)

1 Combine pork, beer, barbecue sauce and chili powder in large saucepan over medium-high heat; bring to a boil. Reduce heat to medium-low. Cover; simmer 50 minutes or until pork is tender, stirring occasionally. Transfer pork to large bowl; shred using two forks.

2 Bring sauce to a boil over medium-high heat; boil 8 to 10 minutes or until thickened. Add ¾ cup sauce to shredded pork; discard remaining sauce.

3 Place tortillas on work surface. Layer bottom half of each tortilla evenly with pork and cheese. Fold top halves of tortillas over filling to form semicircle.

4 Heat large nonstick skillet over medium heat. Add two quesadillas; cook 6 to 8 minutes or until golden and cheese is melted, turning once. Transfer to cutting board. Cut into six wedges. Repeat with remaining quesadillas. Serve with salsa, sour cream and cilantro, if desired.

FILET MIGNON WITH BLUE CHEESE SAUCE

Makes 4 servings

4 filet mignon steaks (4 ounces each), trimmed

¼ teaspoon salt

¼ teaspoon black pepper, plus additional for garnish

⅓ cup chicken broth

⅓ cup evaporated milk

2 teaspoons all-purpose flour

3 tablespoons crumbled blue cheese

1 Spray large skillet with nonstick cooking spray; heat over medium-high heat. Sprinkle steaks on both sides with salt and ¼ teaspoon pepper.

2 Add steaks to skillet; cook 5 minutes on each side or until desired doneness. Remove from pan; cover with foil to keep warm.

3 Combine broth, milk and flour in small saucepan, stirring with a whisk. Heat over medium-high heat and bring to a boil, stirring constantly. Cook 45 seconds or until thickened. Remove from heat. Stir in cheese; serve over steaks. Sprinkle with additional black pepper, if desired.

CHICKEN PARMESAN

Makes 4 servings

½ cup all-purpose flour

¼ teaspoon salt

¼ teaspoon ground black pepper

¼ cup milk

2 eggs

¾ cup CREAM OF WHEAT® Hot Cereal (Instant, 1-minute, 2½-minute or 10-minute cook time), uncooked

¾ cup grated Parmesan cheese

¼ cup olive oil

4 boneless skinless chicken breasts (about 1 pound)

2 cups pasta sauce, divided

1½ cups shredded mozzarella cheese, divided

Grated Parmesan cheese (optional)

1 Preheat oven to 350°F. Blend flour, salt and pepper in shallow bowl; set aside. Combine milk and eggs in second shallow bowl; set aside. Blend Cream of Wheat and ¾ cup Parmesan cheese in third shallow bowl; set aside.

2 Heat oil in large skillet over medium heat. Flatten chicken breasts slightly to uniform thickness. Dip each chicken breast into flour mixture, covering both sides evenly; shake off excess flour. Dip into egg mixture, covering both sides evenly. Dip into Cream of Wheat mixture, covering both sides evenly; shake off excess coating.

3 Place chicken into skillet. Cook 4 minutes or until edges begin to brown. Turn chicken over and cook 5 minutes longer until lightly browned. Remove chicken from skillet.

4 Spread 1 cup pasta sauce in bottom of casserole dish; place chicken on top. Sprinkle ¾ cup mozzarella cheese over chicken and top with remaining 1 cup pasta sauce. Sprinkle on remaining ¾ cup mozzarella cheese. Bake 30 minutes. Remove from oven and garnish with Parmesan cheese, if desired.

TIP: For more variety in your menus, substitute peeled eggplant or sliced pork tenderloin for the chicken.

CHEESY TUNA PIE

Makes 6 servings

2 cups cooked rice

2 cans (6 ounces each) tuna, drained and flaked

1 cup mayonnaise

1 cup (4 ounces) shredded Cheddar cheese

½ cup sour cream

½ cup thinly sliced celery

1 can (4 ounces) sliced black olives

2 tablespoons dried minced onion

1 refrigerated pie crust (half of 15-ounce package)

1 Preheat oven to 350°F. Spray 9-inch deep-dish pie plate with nonstick cooking spray.

2 Combine rice, tuna, mayonnaise, cheese, sour cream, celery, olives and onion in medium bowl; mix well. Spoon into prepared plate. Top with pie crust; press edge of crust into pie plate to seal. Cut slits in top of crust with tip of knife.

3 Bake 20 minutes or until filling is bubbly and crust is lightly browned.

VEGETARIAN FAVORITES

CLASSIC MACARONI AND CHEESE

Makes 8 servings

- **2 cups uncooked elbow macaroni**
- **¼ cup (½ stick) butter**
- **¼ cup all-purpose flour**
- **2½ cups whole milk**
- **1 teaspoon salt**
- **⅛ teaspoon black pepper**
- **4 cups (16 ounces) shredded Colby-Jack cheese**

1 Cook pasta according to package directions until al dente; drain.

2 Melt butter in large saucepan over medium heat. Add flour; whisk until well blended and bubbly. Gradually add milk, salt and pepper, whisking until blended. Cook and stir until milk begins to bubble. Add cheese, 1 cup at a time; cook and stir until cheese is melted and sauce is smooth.

3 Add cooked pasta; stir gently until blended. Cook until heated through.

MARGHERITA PIZZA
WITH QUINOA CRUST
Makes 4 servings

1 **cup uncooked quinoa**

⅓ **cup water, plus additional for soaking**

1 **teaspoon baking powder**

¾ **teaspoon kosher salt**

1 **tablespoon olive oil, plus drizzle for serving**

½ **cup marinara sauce**

1 **ball (8 ounces) fresh mozzarella cheese, cut into ¼-inch-thick slices**

Fresh basil leaves, flaky sea salt and freshly ground black pepper (optional)

1 Place quinoa in medium bowl; cover with 1 inch of water. Cover bowl; let soak 8 hours or overnight at room temperature. Rinse well and drain.

2 Combine soaked quinoa, ⅓ cup water, baking powder and salt in bowl of food processor fitted with blade attachment. Process 2 minutes or until completely smooth, stopping occasionally to scrape down sides of bowl as needed.

3 Preheat oven to 450°F. Cover bottom of 10-inch springform pan with foil. Brush with 1 tablespoon oil. Attach sides of pan. Pour quinoa mixture in pan, using spatula to spread over bottom. Bake 10 to 12 minutes or until quinoa is golden on sides and bottom.

4 Remove pan from oven. Remove sides of pan. Spread marinara sauce evenly over crust. Top with cheese; return to oven. Bake 10 minutes or until cheese is melted and bottom of crust is golden brown.

5 Slide pizza onto large cutting board. Top with basil and additional oil. Sprinkle with sea salt and pepper, if desired. Slice and serve immediately.

SPICY POLENTA CHEESE BITES

Makes 32 appetizers

3 cups water

1 cup corn grits or cornmeal

½ teaspoon salt

¼ teaspoon chili powder

1 tablespoon butter

¼ cup minced onion or shallot

1 tablespoon minced jalapeño pepper*

½ cup (2 ounces) shredded sharp Cheddar or fontina cheese

Jalapeño peppers can sting and irritate the skin, so wear rubber gloves when handling peppers and do not touch your eyes.

1 Grease 8-inch square baking pan. Bring water to a boil in large nonstick saucepan over high heat. Gradually add grits, stirring constantly. Reduce heat to low; cook and stir until grits are tender and water is absorbed. Stir in salt and chili powder. Remove from heat.

2 Melt butter in small saucepan over medium-high heat. Add onion and jalapeño pepper; cook and stir 3 to 5 minutes or until tender. Stir into grits; mix well. Spread in prepared pan. Let stand 1 hour or until cool and firm.

3 Preheat broiler. Cut polenta into 16 squares. Arrange squares on nonstick baking sheet; sprinkle with cheese. Broil 4 inches from heat source 5 minutes or until cheese is melted and slightly browned. Cut squares in half. Serve warm or at room temperature.

TIP: For spicier flavor, add ⅛ teaspoon red pepper flakes to the onion mixture.

HEARTY VEGETARIAN
MAC AND CHEESE

Makes 6 servings

1 can (about 14 ounces) stewed tomatoes, undrained

1½ cups prepared Alfredo sauce

1½ cups (6 ounces) shredded mozzarella cheese, divided

8 ounces whole grain pasta (medium shells or penne shape), cooked and drained

7 ounces Italian-flavored vegetarian sausage links, cut into ¼-inch slices

¾ cup fresh basil leaves, thinly sliced and divided

½ cup vegetable broth

½ teaspoon salt

2 tablespoons grated Parmesan cheese

SLOW COOKER DIRECTIONS

Coat inside of slow cooker with nonstick cooking spray. Add tomatoes, Alfredo sauce, 1 cup mozzarella cheese, pasta, sausage, ½ cup basil, broth and salt to slow cooker; stir to blend. Top with remaining ½ cup mozzarella cheese and Parmesan cheese. Cover; cook on LOW 3½ hours or on HIGH 2 hours. Top with remaining ¼ cup basil.

SPICY MEXICAN FRITTATA

Makes 4 servings

1 **fresh jalapeño pepper***

1 **clove garlic**

1 **medium tomato, peeled, halved, quartered and seeded**

½ **teaspoon ground coriander**

½ **teaspoon chili powder**

Nonstick cooking spray

½ **cup chopped onion**

1 **cup frozen corn**

6 **egg whites**

2 **eggs**

¼ **cup milk**

¼ **teaspoon salt**

¼ **teaspoon black pepper**

¼ **cup (1 ounce) shredded farmer or mozzarella cheese**

*Jalapeño peppers can sting and irritate the skin, so wear rubber gloves when handling peppers and do not touch your eyes.

1 Place jalapeño pepper and garlic in food processor or blender; process until finely chopped. Add tomato, coriander and chili powder. Cover; process until tomato is almost smooth.

2 Spray large skillet with cooking spray; heat over medium heat. Add onion; cook and stir 5 to 7 minutes until tender. Stir in tomato mixture and corn; cook 3 to 4 minutes or until liquid is almost evaporated, stirring occasionally.

3 Combine egg whites, eggs, milk, salt and black pepper in medium bowl. Add egg mixture all at once to skillet. Cook, without stirring, 2 minutes or until eggs begin to set. Run large spoon around edge of skillet, lifting eggs for even cooking. Remove skillet from heat when eggs are almost set but surface is still moist.

4 Sprinkle with cheese. Cover; let stand 3 to 4 minutes or until surface is set and cheese is melted. Cut into four wedges.

FRIED GREEN TOMATO PARMESAN

Makes 4 servings

2 cans (15 ounces each) tomato sauce

4 green tomatoes, thickly sliced into 3 slices each

½ teaspoon salt, divided

Black pepper

½ cup all-purpose flour

1 teaspoon Italian seasoning

2 eggs

2 tablespoons water

1½ cups panko bread crumbs

4 tablespoons olive oil

½ cup shredded Parmesan cheese

Shredded fresh basil

Hot cooked spaghetti

1 Preheat oven to 350°F. Spread 1 cup tomato sauce in 9-inch square baking dish. Sprinkle one side of tomatoes with ¼ teaspoon salt; season lightly with pepper.

2 Combine flour, Italian seasoning and remaining ¼ teaspoon salt in shallow bowl. Whisk eggs and water in another shallow bowl. Place panko in third shallow bowl. Coat tomatoes with flour mixture. Dip in egg mixture. Dredge in panko, pressing onto all sides.

3 Heat 2 tablespoons oil in large skillet over medium-high heat. Add half of tomatoes; cook 3 minutes per side or until panko is golden brown. Arrange tomatoes in single layer in sauce in baking dish. Sprinkle 1 teaspoon cheese on each tomato; spread ½ cup sauce over tomatoes. Heat remaining 2 tablespoons oil in same skillet; cook remaining tomatoes 3 minutes per side until coating is golden brown. Stagger tomatoes in second layer over tomatoes in baking dish. Top each tomato with 1 teaspoon cheese and spread 1 cup sauce over top. Sprinkle with remaining cheese.

4 Bake 20 minutes or until cheese is melted and sauce is heated through. Heat remaining tomato sauce. Serve tomatoes with basil, spaghetti and sauce.

CHEESE SOUFFLÉ

Makes 4 servings

¼ cup (½ stick) butter

¼ cup sweet rice flour (mochiko)

1½ cups milk, warmed to room temperature

¼ teaspoon salt

¼ teaspoon ground red pepper

⅛ teaspoon black pepper

6 eggs, separated

1 cup (4 ounces) shredded Cheddar cheese

Pinch cream of tartar (optional)

1 Preheat oven to 375°F. Grease four 2-cup soufflé dishes or one 2-quart soufflé dish.

2 Melt butter in large saucepan over medium-low heat. Add rice flour; whisk 2 minutes or until mixture just begins to color. Gradually whisk in milk. Add salt, red pepper and black pepper; whisk until mixture comes to a boil and thickens. Remove from heat. Stir in egg yolks, one at a time, and cheese.

3 Beat egg whites and cream of tartar in large bowl with electric mixer at high speed until stiff peaks form.

4 Gently fold egg whites into cheese mixture until almost combined. (Some streaks of white should remain.) Transfer mixture to prepared dishes.

5 Bake small soufflés about 20 minutes (30 to 40 minutes for large soufflé) or until puffed and browned and skewer inserted into center comes out moist but clean. Serve immediately.

SPINACH AND FETA FARRO STUFFED PEPPERS

1 tablespoon olive oil

1 package (5 ounces) baby spinach

½ cup sliced green onions (about 4)

2 cloves garlic, crushed

1 tablespoon chopped fresh oregano

1 package (8.8 ounces) quick-cooking farro, prepared according to package directions using vegetable broth in place of water

1 can (about 14 ounces) petite diced tomatoes, drained

⅛ teaspoon black pepper

1 container (4 ounces) crumbled feta cheese, divided

3 large bell peppers, halved lengthwise, cores and ribs removed

1 Preheat oven to 350°F.

2 Heat oil in large skillet over medium-high heat. Add spinach, green onions, garlic and oregano; cook and stir 3 minutes. Stir in farro, tomatoes, black pepper and ½ cup cheese.

3 Spoon farro mixture into bell pepper halves (about ¾ cup each); place in shallow baking pan. Pour ¼ cup water into bottom of pan; cover with foil.

4 Bake 30 minutes or until bell peppers are crisp-tender and filling is heated through. Sprinkle with remaining cheese.

THREE-CHEESE MANICOTTI

Makes 6 servings

1 cup sliced cremini mushrooms

2 cups pasta sauce (without meat)

1 cup ricotta cheese

¼ cup grated Parmesan cheese

1 egg

1 tablespoon chopped fresh basil, plus additional for garnish

⅛ teaspoon salt

¼ teaspoon black pepper

6 cooked manicotti shells

¼ cup (1 ounce) shredded mozzarella cheese

1 Preheat oven to 350°F. Spray large skillet with nonstick cooking spray. Add mushrooms; cook over medium heat 5 minutes or until tender. Stir in pasta sauce. Spread ½ cup sauce mixture in bottom of 11×7-inch glass baking dish.

2 Combine ricotta cheese, Parmesan cheese, egg, 1 tablespoon basil, salt and pepper in medium bowl. Spoon about ¼ cup mixture evenly into manicotti shells. Place filled shells in baking dish (they should fit snugly). Spoon remaining pasta sauce over manicotti. Cover dish loosely with foil.

3 Bake 28 to 30 minutes or until sauce is bubbly. Remove foil and sprinkle with mozzarella cheese. Bake 5 to 10 minutes or until cheese is melted. Let stand 5 minutes before serving. Garnish with additional basil.

ASIAGO AND ASPARAGUS RISOTTO-STYLE RICE

Makes 4 servings

2 cups chopped onions

1 cup uncooked converted rice

2 cloves garlic, minced

1 can (about 14 ounces) vegetable broth

½ pound asparagus spears, trimmed and cut into 1-inch pieces

¾ cup half-and-half, divided

½ cup (about 4 ounces) shredded Asiago cheese, plus additional for garnish

¼ cup (½ stick) butter, cut into small pieces

2 ounces pine nuts or slivered almonds, toasted*

1 teaspoon salt

*To toast pine nuts, cook and stir in small skillet over medium heat 1 to 2 minutes or until lightly browned.

SLOW COOKER DIRECTIONS

1 Combine onions, rice, garlic and broth in slow cooker; stir until well blended. Cover; cook on HIGH 2 hours or until rice is done.

2 Stir in asparagus and ½ cup half-and-half. Cover; cook on HIGH 20 to 30 minutes or until asparagus is crisp-tender.

3 Stir in ½ cup cheese, butter, pine nuts and salt; cover and let stand 5 minutes to allow cheese to melt slightly. Fluff with fork and garnish with additional cheese before serving.

TIP: Risotto is a classic creamy rice dish of northern Italy. It can be made with a wide variety of ingredients; fresh vegetables and cheeses such as Asiago work especially well in risottos. Parmesan cheese, shellfish, dry white wine and herbs are also popular additions.

CHEESY STUFFED POBLANO PEPPERS

Makes 4 servings

3 tablespoons olive oil, divided

1 cup frozen corn, thawed

1 cup diced red onion, divided

¾ cup (3 ounces) crumbled queso blanco cheese

½ cup (2 ounces) shredded Monterey Jack cheese

¼ cup minced fresh cilantro

2 teaspoons minced garlic, divided

4 poblano or green bell peppers

2 medium tomatoes, seeded and diced

Juice of 1 lime

Salt and black pepper

1 Preheat oven to 450°F. Heat 1 tablespoon oil in small skillet over medium-high heat. Add corn and ½ cup onion; cook and stir 5 minutes. Remove to large bowl. Add cheeses, cilantro and 1 teaspoon garlic; mix well.

2 Make two long slits on front of each pepper to create flap. Lift flap; remove and discard seeds and ribs. Divide corn mixture evenly among peppers. Replace flap; secure with wooden skewer, if desired. Place stuffed peppers in baking dish. Brush skins with 1 tablespoon oil.

3 Roast peppers 15 to 20 minutes or until peppers are wrinkled and filling is melted. Meanwhile, combine tomatoes, remaining ½ cup onion, lime juice, remaining 1 tablespoon oil, 1 teaspoon garlic, salt and black pepper in medium bowl. Serve tomato mixture with peppers.

CHEESE RAVIOLI
WITH PUMPKIN SAUCE

Makes 6 servings

- ⅓ **cup sliced green onions**
- 1 **to 2 cloves garlic, minced**
- ½ **teaspoon whole fennel seeds**
- 1 **cup evaporated milk**
- 1 **tablespoon all-purpose flour**
- ¼ **teaspoon salt**
- ⅛ **teaspoon black pepper**
- ½ **cup solid-pack pumpkin**
- 2 **packages (9 ounces each) uncooked refrigerated cheese ravioli**
- 2 **tablespoons grated Parmesan cheese (optional)**

1 Spray medium nonstick saucepan with nonstick cooking spray. Cook and stir green onions, garlic and fennel seeds over medium heat 3 minutes or until green onions are tender.

2 Combine evaporated milk, flour, salt and pepper in small bowl until smooth; stir into saucepan. Bring to a boil over high heat; boil until thickened, stirring constantly. Stir in pumpkin; reduce heat to low.

3 Meanwhile, cook ravioli according to package directions, omitting salt; drain. Divide ravioli evenly among six plates. Top each with equal amount of pumpkin sauce; sprinkle with cheese, if desired. Serve immediately.

FRESH VEGETABLE CASSEROLE

Makes 4 to 6 servings

8 small new potatoes

8 baby carrots

1 head cauliflower, broken into florets

4 stalks asparagus, cut into 1-inch pieces

3 tablespoons butter

3 tablespoons all-purpose flour

2 cups milk

Salt and black pepper

¾ cup (3 ounces) shredded Cheddar cheese

Chopped fresh cilantro or parsley

1 Preheat oven to 350°F. Grease 2-quart casserole. Steam potatoes, carrots, cauliflower and asparagus in steamer basket over boiling water 5 to 7 minutes or until crisp-tender. Arrange vegetables in prepared casserole.

2 Melt butter in medium saucepan over medium heat. Stir in flour until smooth. Slowly whisk in milk; bring to a boil. Cook and stir 2 minutes or until thickened and bubbly. Season with salt and pepper. Stir in cheese until melted. Pour over vegetables; sprinkle with cilantro.

3 Bake 15 minutes or until heated through.

THREE-CHEESE MACARONI AND QUINOA

Makes 4 servings

- 4 tablespoons (½ stick) butter, divided
- ½ cup panko bread crumbs
- 2 quarts water
- 1 teaspoon salt, divided
- 6 ounces uncooked whole grain elbow macaroni (1½ cups)
- ½ cup uncooked quinoa, preferably the white grain variety
- 2 tablespoons all-purpose flour
- 1 cup milk
- 1 cup (4 ounces) shredded sharp Cheddar cheese
- 1 cup (4 ounces) shredded Monterey Jack cheese
- ¼ cup grated Parmesan cheese

OPTIONAL GARNISHES

- 1 green onion, finely chopped
- 2 tablespoons fresh parsley
- ⅓ cup diced fresh tomato

1 Melt 2 tablespoons butter in 3-quart saucepan over medium heat. Add panko; cook and stir 1 to 2 minutes or until golden. Place in small bowl; set aside.

2 Combine water and ½ teaspoon salt in large saucepan; bring to a boil over high heat. Stir in macaroni and quinoa; boil 10 minutes. Drain in fine-mesh strainer. Place in large serving bowl.

3 Melt remaining 2 tablespoons butter in saucepan over medium heat. Whisk in flour; cook 1 minute without browning. Gradually whisk in milk and remaining ½ teaspoon salt; cook 5 minutes or until very thick. Stir in Cheddar and Monterey Jack cheeses until melted. Pour over macaroni mixture.

4 Top with Parmesan cheese and panko. Garnish as desired.

SUBSTITUTION: For a spicy flavor, try Pepper Jack cheese in place of the Monterey Jack.

BUON GIORNO FRITTATA

Makes 6 servings

- **4** eggs, beaten
- **2** egg whites, beaten
- **¼** cup shredded fresh basil
- **2** tablespoons low-fat milk
- **¼** teaspoon salt
- **⅛** teaspoon black pepper
- **2** teaspoons olive oil
- **2** cups halved and sliced zucchini
- **1** cup diced yellow onions
- **1** can (6 ounces) California Ripe Olives, drained and halved
- **½** cup roasted red bell peppers, sliced into ¼-inch strips
- **¼** cup grated fontina or Parmesan cheese

1 Preheat oven to 400°F. In a medium-sized mixing bowl, whisk together eggs, egg whites, basil, milk, salt and pepper. Set aside.

2 Heat oil in a 10-inch oven-proof skillet over medium heat. Add zucchini and onions and cook for 5 to 6 minutes or until tender. Mix in 1 cup of California Ripe Olives and red bell peppers. Remove from heat and stir into egg mixture.

3 Pour egg and vegetable mixture back into pan. Turn heat to medium-high and cook for 3 to 5 minutes until eggs are set on the bottom. Sprinkle the top of the frittata with grated cheese and remaining California Ripe Olives. Place frittata in oven for 13 to 15 minutes or until cooked through.

4 Cool slightly and cut into 6 wedges.

SERVING SUGGESTION: Serve with crusty country bread.

California Olive Committee

BROCCOLI & CHEESE
STUFFED SHELLS

Makes 6 servings

- 1 container (15 ounces) ricotta cheese
- 1 package (10 ounces) frozen chopped broccoli, thawed and well drained
- 1 cup shredded mozzarella cheese (about 4 ounces)
- ⅓ cup grated Parmesan cheese
- ¼ teaspoon black pepper
- 18 jumbo shell-shaped pasta, cooked and drained
- 1 jar (24 ounces) Prego® Chunky Garden Combination Italian Sauce

1 Stir the ricotta cheese, broccoli, ½ **cup** of the mozzarella cheese, Parmesan cheese and black pepper in a medium bowl. Spoon **about 2 tablespoons** of the cheese mixture into **each** shell.

2 Spread **1 cup** of the Italian sauce in a 13×9×2-inch shallow baking dish. Place the filled shells on the sauce. Pour the remaining sauce over the shells. Sprinkle with the remaining mozzarella cheese.

3 Bake at 400°F. for 25 minutes or until it's hot and bubbling.

KITCHEN TIP: To save time, thaw the broccoli in the microwave on HIGH for 4 minutes.

GANNAT (FRENCH CHEESE BREAD)

Makes 1 loaf

3 to 6 tablespoons warm water (105° to 115°F)

1 package (¼ ounce) active dry yeast

1 teaspoon sugar

2½ cups all-purpose flour

¼ cup (½ stick) butter, at room temperature

1 teaspoon salt

2 eggs

4 ounces Emmentaler Swiss, Gruyère, sharp Cheddar or Swiss cheese, shredded

1 teaspoon vegetable oil

1 Combine 3 tablespoons water, yeast and sugar in small bowl. Stir to dissolve yeast; let stand 5 minutes or until bubbly.

2 Place flour, butter and salt in food processor or blender; process 15 seconds or until mixed. Add yeast mixture and eggs; process 15 seconds or until blended.

3 With processor running, very slowly drizzle just enough remaining water through feed tube so dough forms a ball that cleans the sides of the bowl. Process until ball turns around bowl about 25 times. Turn off processor and let dough stand 1 to 2 minutes.

4 Turn on processor and gradually drizzle in enough remaining water to make dough soft, smooth and satiny but not sticky. Process until dough turns around bowl about 15 times.

5 Turn dough onto lightly floured surface. Shape into a ball and place in lightly greased bowl, turning to grease top. Cover loosely with plastic wrap; let stand in warm place (85°F) 1 hour or until doubled in size.

6 Punch down dough. Place dough on lightly greased surface; knead cheese into dough. Roll or pat into 8-inch circle. Place in well greased 9-inch round cake or pie pan. Brush with oil. Let stand in warm place about 45 minutes or until doubled in size.

7 Preheat oven to 375°F. Bake 30 to 35 minutes or until browned and bread sounds hollow when tapped. Remove immediately from pan; cool on wire rack.

MEXICAN-STYLE RICE AND CHEESE

Makes 6 to 8 servings

1 can (about 15 ounces)
   Mexican-style beans

1 can (about 14 ounces)
   diced tomatoes with
   green chiles

2 cups (8 ounces)
   shredded Monterey
   Jack or Colby cheese,
   divided

1½ cups uncooked
   converted long
   grain rice

1 large onion, finely
   chopped

½ (8-ounce) package
   cream cheese

3 cloves garlic, minced

SLOW COOKER DIRECTIONS

1 Spray inside of slow cooker with nonstick cooking spray. Combine beans, tomatoes, 1 cup Monterey Jack cheese, rice, onion, cream cheese and garlic in slow cooker; mix well.

2 Cover; cook on LOW 6 to 8 hours. Sprinkle with remaining 1 cup Monterey Jack cheese just before serving.

MEDITERRANEAN RED POTATOES

Makes 4 servings

3 medium red potatoes, cut into 1-inch pieces

⅔ cup fresh or frozen pearl onions

Garlic-flavored cooking spray

¾ teaspoon Italian seasoning

¼ teaspoon black pepper

1 small tomato, seeded and chopped

2 ounces (½ cup) crumbled feta cheese

2 tablespoons chopped black olives

SLOW COOKER DIRECTIONS

1 Place potatoes and onions in 1½-quart soufflé dish. Spray potatoes and onions with cooking spray; toss to coat. Add Italian seasoning and pepper; mix well. Cover dish tightly with foil.

2 Tear off three 18×3-inch strips of heavy-duty foil. Cross strips to resemble wheel spokes. Place soufflé dish in center of strips. Pull foil strips up and over dish to make handles and place dish into slow cooker.

3 Pour hot water into slow cooker to about 1½ inches from top of soufflé dish. Cover; cook on LOW 7 to 8 hours.

4 Use foil handles to lift dish out of slow cooker. Stir tomato, cheese and olives into potato mixture.

QUATTRO FORMAGGIO PIZZA

Makes 4 servings

½ **cup prepared pizza or marinara sauce**

1 **(12-inch) prepared pizza crust**

4 **ounces shaved or thinly sliced provolone cheese**

2 **ounces Asiago or brick cheese, thinly sliced**

1 **cup (4 ounces) shredded smoked or regular mozzarella cheese**

¼ **cup grated Parmesan or Romano cheese**

Red pepper flakes (optional)

1 Preheat oven to 450°F. Spread pizza sauce evenly over pizza crust; place on baking sheet.

2 Sprinkle with provolone and Asiago cheeses; top with mozzarella and Parmesan cheeses. Bake 14 minutes or until pizza crust is golden brown and cheeses are melted. Cut into wedges. Serve with red pepper flakes, if desired.

SERVING SUGGESTION: Serve with a tossed green salad.

SWEET POTATO NOODLES WITH BLUE CHEESE AND WALNUTS

Makes 2 servings

2 sweet potatoes
  (1½ pounds)

¼ cup chopped walnuts

1 tablespoon olive oil

2 cloves garlic, minced

¼ cup whipping cream

1 package (5 ounces)
  baby spinach

¼ cup crumbled blue
  cheese

¼ teaspoon salt

¼ teaspoon black pepper

1 Spiral sweet potatoes with thin ribbon blade. Loosely pile on cutting board and cut in an X. Heat large nonstick skillet over medium-high heat. Add walnuts; cook and stir 3 to 4 minutes until toasted. Remove to plate; cool completely.

2 Heat oil in same skillet over medium-high heat. Add potatoes; cook and stir 10 minutes or until potatoes are desired doneness, adding water by tablespoonfuls if potatoes are browning too quickly.

3 Add garlic; cook and stir 30 seconds. Add cream and spinach; cook and stir 1 minute or until cream is absorbed and spinach is wilted. Transfer to bowls; top with walnuts and cheese. Season with salt and pepper.

INDEX

ACKNOWLEDGMENTS

The publisher would like to thank the companies and organizations listed below for the use of their recipes and photographs in this publication.

The Beef Checkoff

California Olive Committee

Campbell Soup Company

**Cream of Wheat® Cereal,
A Division of B&G Foods North America, Inc.**

Ortega®, A Division of B&G Foods North America, Inc.

Reckitt Benckiser LLC.

Sargento® Foods Inc.

Unilever

METRIC CONVERSION CHART

VOLUME MEASUREMENTS (dry)

$1/8$ teaspoon = 0.5 mL
$1/4$ teaspoon = 1 mL
$1/2$ teaspoon = 2 mL
$3/4$ teaspoon = 4 mL
1 teaspoon = 5 mL
1 tablespoon = 15 mL
2 tablespoons = 30 mL
$1/4$ cup = 60 mL
$1/3$ cup = 75 mL
$1/2$ cup = 125 mL
$2/3$ cup = 150 mL
$3/4$ cup = 175 mL
1 cup = 250 mL
2 cups = 1 pint = 500 mL
3 cups = 750 mL
4 cups = 1 quart = 1 L

VOLUME MEASUREMENTS (fluid)

1 fluid ounce (2 tablespoons) = 30 mL
4 fluid ounces ($1/2$ cup) = 125 mL
8 fluid ounces (1 cup) = 250 mL
12 fluid ounces ($1 1/2$ cups) = 375 mL
16 fluid ounces (2 cups) = 500 mL

WEIGHTS (mass)

$1/2$ ounce = 15 g
1 ounce = 30 g
3 ounces = 90 g
4 ounces = 120 g
8 ounces = 225 g
10 ounces = 285 g
12 ounces = 360 g
16 ounces = 1 pound = 450 g

DIMENSIONS

$1/16$ inch = 2 mm
$1/8$ inch = 3 mm
$1/4$ inch = 6 mm
$1/2$ inch = 1.5 cm
$3/4$ inch = 2 cm
1 inch = 2.5 cm

OVEN TEMPERATURES

250°F = 120°C
275°F = 140°C
300°F = 150°C
325°F = 160°C
350°F = 180°C
375°F = 190°C
400°F = 200°C
425°F = 220°C
450°F = 230°C

BAKING PAN SIZES

Utensil	Size in Inches/Quarts	Metric Volume	Size in Centimeters
Baking or Cake Pan (square or rectangular)	8×8×2	2 L	20×20×5
	9×9×2	2.5 L	23×23×5
	12×8×2	3 L	30×20×5
	13×9×2	3.5 L	33×23×5
Loaf Pan	8×4×3	1.5 L	20×10×7
	9×5×3	2 L	23×13×7
Round Layer Cake Pan	8×1½	1.2 L	20×4
	9×1½	1.5 L	23×4
Pie Plate	8×1¼	750 mL	20×3
	9×1¼	1 L	23×3
Baking Dish or Casserole	1 quart	1 L	—
	1½ quart	1.5 L	—
	2 quart	2 L	—